New England Fish Species

Game Fish & Panfish

Billy Grinslott & Kinsey Marie Books

ISBN - 9781968228620

Banded Sunfish got their name because they have darker lines that run vertically on their sides. They also have a rounded tail with spots on their body, tail and fins. Banded sunfish are typically only about 2 inches long, making them one of the smallest sunfish. Their small size makes them vulnerable to larger fish, so they thrive in protected areas. Banded sunfish prefer slow-moving, vegetated waters like swamps, ponds, and backwaters of creeks.

The Green Sunfish is blue green in color. It has yellow flecks on both its scales and some parts of its sides. The Green Sunfish also has broken blue stripes which is why some people confuse it with the Bluegill. Green Sunfish are very adaptable. They can live in any body of water that has vegetation or weeds. Green sunfish are opportunistic feeders, consuming insects, small fish, and other invertebrates.

The bluegill also considered a sunfish is the most popular fish to fish for. They are called pan fish because they are about the size of a frying pan. Bluegills love to eat insects and bugs. They have good vision and rely on their keen eyesight to feed. Three types in this group are the Bluegill, Sunfish, and Pumpkinseed.

The Redbreast sunfish has a red-yellow chest and belly with rusty brown spots on their body. The species is known for its distinctive grunting vocalizations, which are produced by grinding their teeth together. Redbreast sunfish can survive in oxygen-poor environments by using their gills to extract oxygen from air bubbles trapped in aquatic vegetation.

Hybrid sunfish are fast-growing crosses between two different sunfish species, most commonly a male bluegill and a female green sunfish. They possess mixed traits from parents, typically featuring the body shape of a bluegill with the larger mouth and coloration of a green sunfish. They are highly aggressive, making them excellent, easy-to-catch gamefish for children and beginners. They exhibit rapid growth rates, often reaching 1 pound or more quickly.

The Pumpkinseed is also known as pond perch, sun perch, and punky's sunfish. It can be found in numerous lakes, ponds, and rivers. It is their body shape resembling the seed of a pumpkin, that inspired their name. Pumpkinseed sunfish have speckles on their orangish colored sides and back, with a yellow to orange belly and chest. They are active during the day and rest at night near the bottom or in shelter areas.

White perch grow seven to ten inches in length and rarely weigh more than one pound. They have a silvery body with faint lines on the sides. The white perch is an opportunistic feeder. Young feed primarily on zooplankton and adults feed on aquatic insect larvae, minnows and fish eggs. White Perch is a euryhaline species, inhabiting fresh, brackish and coastal waters. The biggest white perch caught in New England is a 3 lb. 8 oz. (18-inch) fish caught in the Wachusett Reservoir, Massachusetts.

The two most famous perches are the common perch and the yellow perch. The yellow perch has a brilliant greenish yellow color with orange fins. The yellow perch is the biggest one and can grow to a size of 18 inches. It's also known as the jumbo perch. The other type of perch is the white perch. The biggest yellow perch caught in the New England region was a 2-pound, 13-ounce fish caught in Connecticut.

Alewives are anadromous fish that migrate from the ocean to freshwater rivers and streams to spawn. They are small, silvery herring-like fish with a saw-edged belly and a forked tail. Alewives have a distinctive saw-edge on their belly, formed by modified scales called scutes. This feature is used for protection and is also what gives them the nickname saw bellies. While most alewives are anadromous, there are also populations that have become landlocked.

Fallfish are the largest native minnow species in eastern North America, often reaching 15-18 inches in length and weighing over 2 pounds, inhabiting clear, rocky streams. They are known for building massive, pyramid-shaped nests from rocks, with males creating structures that can reach 6 feet in diameter and weigh up to 2 tons. They are silvery with dark-edged scales, a dark stripe along the back, and a large, blunt snout. The biggest Fallfish caught in the New England region was a 3 lb. 8.96 oz fish caught in New Hampshire.

The Rock Bass is not actually a bass but a member of the sunfish family. The biggest Rock Bass ever caught on record weighs about three pounds and was a little over one foot long. Rock bass, like waters with rocky vegetated areas, that's how they got their name.

There are two main types of crappies. The white crappie and the black crappie. They are also members of the sunfish family. The difference between the white and black crappie is one has dark spots and the other has dark lines and is lighter in color. The white crappie has six dorsal fin spines, whereas the black crappie has eight dorsal fin spines. The white crappie can grow bigger and more of the bigger white crappie are caught in North America. The largest crappie recorded in the Northeast is a 4-pound, 7-ounce white crappie.

The sucker fish has the same mouth as a carp. They got their name because their mouth is like a suction cup. They normally are bottom feeders and suck their food from the bottom of the lake. Many people use sucker fish to fish for northern pike and other big game fish. The biggest white sucker caught in the New England region is a 5-pound, 5.4-ounce fish caught in Vermont.

The Longnose Sucker is recognized by its long snout, cylindrical body, and thick, papillose lips. They have a dusky gray green to brown back with a white, underside, and a distinctive long snout that overhangs the mouth. Typically, they grow 12 to 18 inches long and live 8 to 20 years. Longnose suckers are bottom feeders that use their fleshy lips to vacuum up algae, midge larvae, small mollusks, and various aquatic invertebrates.

The black, brown and yellow bullhead are part of the catfish family. They usually only grow to about 10 inches long. They use their whiskers to help find food. The bullhead is the most common member of the catfish family. Bullheads live in the water containing low oxygen levels. They can survive on low oxygen areas, where other fish can't. The largest bullhead caught in the New England region is a 6-pound, 4-ounce yellow bullhead caught in Massachusetts.

The Channel Catfish are the most fished catfish species with around 8 million anglers fishing for them per year. Channel catfish have taste buds all over their body, making them highly sensitive to the taste and smell of food. They also have barbels (whiskers) around their mouths, which are used for sensing and tasting food. They use sound waves to communicate with each other. They can also produce alarm substances to warn other catfish of danger. The biggest Channel Catfish caught in the New England region, in Maine, is a 37-pound 9-ounce fish.

The madtom is a small catfish that is native to the eastern United States. Madtoms are scaleless fishes with eight whisker-like barbels around their mouths used as sensors. The madtom feeds on the bottom at night, using its sensitive barbels, whiskers to touch and taste for food. Its diet consists mostly of aquatic insects.

White catfish are interesting because they are smaller than other common catfish species like channel catfish, they have a wider head and lack the black spots of channel catfish. White catfish are the smallest of the large North American catfish species. The White catfish has white chin barbells, which distinguish it from other species. There are four pairs of barbels, whiskers around the mouth, two on the chin, one at the angle of the mouth, and one behind the nostril. The biggest white catfish caught in the New England region is a 21.3-pound fish caught in Connecticut.

Blue catfish are known for their size, reaching over 100 pounds. Blue catfish, like other catfish, lack scales and have smooth skin. They have barbels (whiskers) around their mouths, which are used for sensing and tasting food. They are generally slate blue on the back and silvery/white on the underside. Blue catfish are not native to New England, but they have established populations along the East Coast, particularly in the Chesapeake Bay watershed.

Bowfins can breathe both air and water, putting them at an advantage in low-oxygen waters. Bowfins are often described as prehistoric relics. This is because species can be traced to fossils from the Cretaceous, Eocene and Jurassic period. The biggest Bowfin (often called dogfish) caught in the New England region is a 14-pound, 8-ounce fish caught in Vermont.

The American shad is the largest species in the herring family. They are known for a delicate, rich flavor, often described as oily or like sardines. They can grow up to 30 inches and weigh up to 12 pounds. They have a metallic blue/green back, silver sides, a deeply forked tail, and a row of dark spots behind the gill flap. They prefer freshwater rivers for spawning and the Atlantic Ocean for feeding, often traveling hundreds of miles upstream. The biggest American shad caught in the New England region, in Massachusetts, weighed 11 pounds, 4 ounces.

The burbot, also known as the eel pout. They get their name because they have a serpent-like or eel-like body. They can wrap their tail around things. There's nothing to worry about if you catch one, they may try to wrap their tail around your arm, but they are harmless. Burbots are adapted to cold water and are found in large, cold rivers, lakes, and reservoirs, primarily preferring freshwater habitats. Burbots are also known as ling, cusk, or eelpout. The biggest burbot caught in the New England region was a 12-pound, 8.48-ounce (35-inch) fish caught in New Hampshire.

The Hybrid Striped Bass is a cross between a male White Bass and a female Striped Bass, known for its broken stripes, deep body, and excellent fighting ability. It's a favorite game fish in many freshwater reservoirs, prized for its aggressive nature, often caught with spoons, jigs, or live bait, especially in cooler months. They are sterile and do not reproduce naturally, so they are stocked in lakes and rivers by state hatcheries. They can grow to significant sizes, often reaching several pounds within three years. The largest recorded hybrid striped bass (wiper) in the New England region is a 17-pound, 12-ounce fish.

Striped bass are often called Stripers. Striped bass live in both salt and fresh water. Striped bass have very sensitive eyes and will seek deep water when the sun is out. Striped bass have a preferred water temperature range of from 55° F to 68° F, and swim to find water of these temperatures. White Bass are related to Striped Bass and have lighter stripes on their sides. The biggest striped bass caught in the New England region is a 81-pound, 14-ounce fish caught in Connecticut.

Sturgeons have sharp spines on their back, so be careful when handling them. Instead of scales, sturgeon skin is covered in bony plates called scutes, which can be very sharp on young sturgeon. Sturgeons have been around since the dinosaur days. Sturgeons mostly live in large, freshwater lakes and rivers. Their average lifespan is 50 to 60 years. The largest sturgeon recorded in the New England region, is a 7-foot-long, 250-pound Atlantic sturgeon caught in the Saco River in Maine.

There are few different species of Gar, the Longnose gar, Short nose and Alligator gar. The Long Nose Gar got its name because of its long mouth that looks like an alligator's mouth. The alligator gar is one of the biggest freshwater fish growing up to 10 feet long. The world record for a catch was set at 327 pounds. The largest gar recorded in the New England region (specifically Vermont) is an 18.6-pound, 54.75-inch Longnose Gar.

The American eel is North America's only freshwater eel, known for its snake-like body, and ability to live in freshwater. They have a Snake-like body, dark on top (green/brown) with yellowish sides and a pale belly. They have a continuous fin that runs along the length of their whole back. They use their whole body to swim and can slither like a snake over the ground and obstacles. They are most active at night and hide during the day, under rocks or burying themselves into the sediment at the bottom. The largest recorded American eels in the New England region was a 10.2-pound, 52-inch fish from Connecticut.

Snakehead fish are known as walking fish, because they can move on land for days by wiggling with their fins and body. They can breathe air with lung-like organs, allowing them to survive out of water for days and even crawl to new water bodies using their fins. They can also burrow into the mud and hibernate during cold weather or dry spells. They thrive in various slow-moving, shallow, vegetated waters, like ponds, swamps, and streams, and can survive in low oxygen levels. The biggest Northern Snakehead caught in the New England region was a 5-pound, 8-ounce, 30-inch fish caught in Massachusetts.

Male freshwater drum also known as sheepshead make a rumbling or grunting sound by contracting muscles along their air bladder walls. They have large, ivory-like ear bones that can be up to an inch in diameter, which Native Americans used as necklaces or bracelets and sometimes referred to as the lucky stones. Freshwater drum are primarily bottom feeders, spending much of their time near the bottom of lakes and rivers in search of food. The largest black drum fish documented in the New England region is a 36.41-pound black drum caught in Connecticut.

Carp have long been an important food fish to humans. Carp are bottom feeders for the most part and their mouth is made like a suction cup, so they can suck food off the bottom. Carp are good for a lake because they help clean the bottom of the lake. The biggest carp caught in the New England region is a 58.05-pound common carp caught in Connecticut.

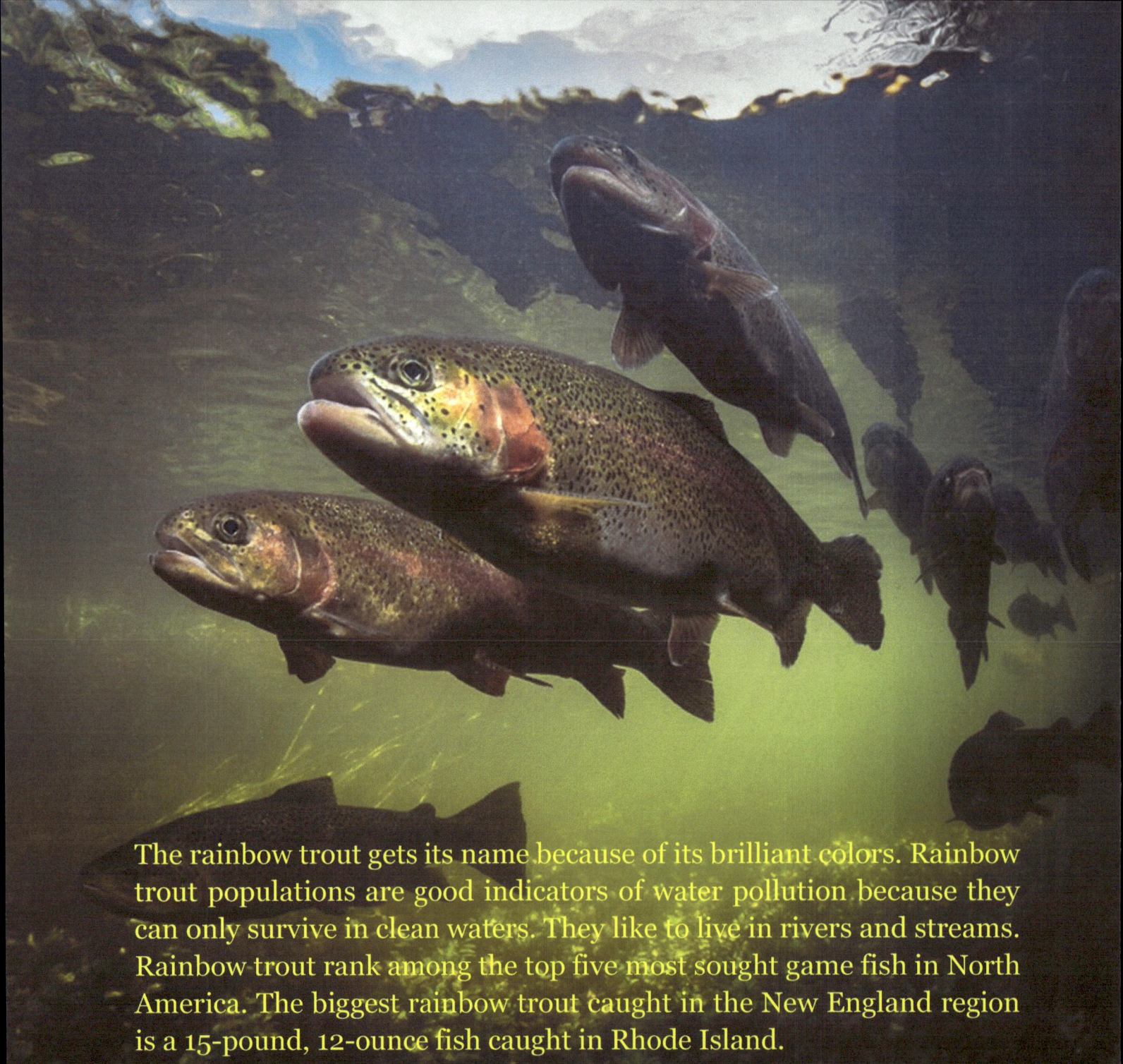

The rainbow trout gets its name because of its brilliant colors. Rainbow trout populations are good indicators of water pollution because they can only survive in clean waters. They like to live in rivers and streams. Rainbow trout rank among the top five most sought game fish in North America. The biggest rainbow trout caught in the New England region is a 15-pound, 12-ounce fish caught in Rhode Island.

The lake trout is one of the biggest of the trout family. The biggest lake trout caught was 72 pounds. Lake trout like to live in lakes that are deep. They like being in the cool water in the deep parts of a lake. They have been reported to live up to 70 years in some Canadian lakes. The biggest lake trout caught in the New England region is a 39.2-pound fish caught in Maine.

Brook trout are characterized by their olive-green bodies with pale, worm-like markings, red spots with bluish halos, and orange-red fins with white and black edges. They can grow up to 12 inches in length. Brook trout are cold-water fish that prefer clean, clear, and cold streams, lakes, and ponds. The largest Brook trout caught in the New England region is a 9-pound, 2-ounce fish taken in Maine.

Brown trout can live up to 20 years. Brown trout have a higher tolerance for warmer waters than either brook or rainbow trout. Brown trout can be found on almost every continent except Antarctica, and many can be found living in the ocean. They have olive-brown, yellow-orange, or silvery sides with a mix of black, red, and orange spots. One of the largest Brown trout documented in New England was an 18-pound, 34-inch fish caught on the Deerfield River.

Tiger trout are known for their aggressive nature and awesome looking tiger-like stripes. Tiger trout are not naturally occurring in the wild, but rather a hybrid created by mixing a female brown trout with a male brook trout. They are stocked in lakes and rivers. Their striking appearance with tiger-like stripes and patterns, makes them easily recognizable. They are known to grow faster than their parent species. For the New England region, the biggest tiger trout officially recorded is a 7.1-pound, 24.5-inch fish caught in Connecticut.

Smallmouth bass have a smaller mouth than the largemouth bass. They also have different markings and are lighter in color. They don't live in most lakes because they prefer living in colder water. They are typically found in the northern states in America because the water is cooler. The current world record smallmouth is an 11-pound, 15-ounce fish. They can be found in lakes, reservoirs, and rivers. The largest Smallmouth bass caught in the New England region is a 8-pound, 2-ounce fish caught in Massachusetts.

The largemouth bass is the most sought-after bass in North America. Largemouth bass live in just about every lake in North America. They have great hearing and can hear a crayfish crawling on the bottom of the lake. The largest largemouth bass caught in the New England region is a 15-pound, 8-ounce fish, caught in Massachusetts.

The walleye got its name because of its white looking eyes. Their eyes collect light, even in low light conditions. This means they can see in the dark. Because they can see in the dark, they mostly feed at night. During the daytime their eyes are very sensitive, so they usually head for deeper water or shady places. Walleye like to live in cooler water and are normally found in the upper part of North America. The largest walleye caught in the New England region is a 15.23-pound fish caught in Connecticut.

Pickerel kind of look like northern pike, but they are not. The Pike is larger in size than the Pickerel. The Pickerel has more spots than the Pike, but the Pike has spots on its fins and pickerel don't. Pickerel has a dark bar beneath their eyes and northern pike don't. Pickerel are also known as gunfish or slime darts. The largest chain pickerel caught in Massachusetts weighed 9 pounds, 5 ounces.

The Redfin Pickerel is a small, solitary freshwater fish in the pike family, typically measuring 10–15 inches and living 8–10 years. They inhabit clear, slow-moving, heavily vegetated streams and swamps. They are ambush predators feeding on small fish, crustaceans, and insects. They are olive to yellowish green with distinct, bright red-orange fins and a dark, backwards-slanting bar beneath the eye.

The Northern Pike is one of the most sought-after fish for anglers. It got its name because it likes to live in cooler water mainly in the northern states of North America. The northern pike is a very aggressive predator. They don't like to live in groups with other fish, they are very territorial and like to live alone. Their behavior is closely affected by weather conditions. The largest Northern Pike caught in the New England region was a 31.2-pound (49-inch) fish caught in Maine.

The muskellunge called the Musky or Muskie for short is one of the biggest game fish in freshwater lakes. The largest on record was 69 pounds, 15 ounces. The Muskie likes to live in cooler water and can be found in most lakes in the upper part of north America. Anglers look at Muskellunges as trophy fish. They are hard to catch. There's a saying that it takes a thousand casts to catch one. The largest recorded pure-strain muskellunge caught in the New England region is a 38-pound, 4-ounce (approx. 52-inch) fish caught in Vermont.

Another breed of the Muskie is the tiger muskie. The tiger muskie is a cross between the northern pike and muskie. They grow larger and faster than normal muskies and northern pikes. The tiger muskie got its name because it has tiger like stripes. Tiger Muskies are very rare and hard to catch. The world record tiger muskie is a massive fish weighing 51 pounds, 3 ounces. The largest recorded tiger muskellunge in the New England region is a 27-pound, 46-inch specimen caught in Massachusetts.

Atlantic salmon are anadromous, meaning they live in both freshwater and saltwater. Atlantic Salmon are present in Massachusetts, primarily as landlocked fish in inland lakes and tributaries rather than sea-run fish. They are known for their impressive leaping abilities, allowing them to jump over waterfalls and obstacles to reach spawning grounds. Atlantic salmon change color when they return to freshwater to spawn, becoming a rusty-bronze color with red markings. The largest Atlantic salmon recorded in the New England region is a 28 lb. 1 oz. fish caught in Maine.

The primary salmon species you'll find are landlocked sockeye salmon, also known as kokanee. These are the non-anadromous form of sockeye salmon, meaning they don't migrate to the ocean. They live their entire lives in freshwater lakes and reservoirs. The largest landlocked salmon ever caught in the New England region was a 22-pound, 8-ounce fish caught in Maine.

Author Page

Billy Grinslott & Kinsey Marie Books

ISBN – 9781968228620

Thanks

www.ingramcontent.com/pod-product-compliance
Lightning Source LLC
Chambersburg PA
CBHW060848270326
41934CB00002B/47